WEST VIRGINIA
THE ALLEGHENY HIGHLANDS

TEXT AND PHOTOGRAPHY BY JIM CLARK
FOREWORD BY VIRGINIA MARIE PETERSON

WESTCLIFFE PUBLISHERS

ENGLEWOOD, COLORADO

ISBN: 1-56579-296-3

PHOTOGRAPHS AND TEXT:
Copyright 1998 Jim Clark. ALL RIGHTS RESERVED.

DESIGNER: Rebecca Finkel, F + P Graphic Design
PRODUCTION MANAGER: Harlene Finn
EDITOR: Sallie Greenwood

PUBLISHED BY:
Westcliffe Publishers, Inc.
P.O. Box 1261
Englewood, Colorado 80150

PRINTED IN
Hong Kong by H & Y Printing Ltd.

LIBRARY OF CONGRESS CATALOGING-IN-PUBLICATION-DATA
Clark, Jim 1953–
    West Virginia : the Allegheny Highlands / photography
and text by Jim Clark : foreword by Virginia Marie Peterson.
        p. cm.
    ISBN 1-56579-296-3
    1. Natural history—West Virginia. 2. Natural history—
Allegheny Mountains. 3. Natural history—West Virginia—
Pictorial works. 4. Natural history—Allegheny Mountains
—Pictorial works. I. Title
QH105.W4C58   1998   98-3437
508.754'8—dc21   CIP

*For more information about other fine books and calendars from
Westcliffe Publishers, please call your local bookstore, contact us
at 1-800-523-3692, or write for our free color catalog.*

FIRST FRONTISPIECE: PASTURE IN SPRING, POCAHONTAS COUNTY
SECOND FRONTISPIECE: AUTUMN, HIGHLAND SCENIC HIGHWAY
THIRD FRONTISPIECE: CASCADE, WILLIAMS RIVER,
MONONGAHELA NATIONAL FOREST
PAGE 5: MAPLE LEAVES, WATOGA STATE PARK
OPPOSITE: SUNSET, HIGHLAND SCENIC HIGHWAY

DEDICATION

For two extraordinary women who

have made the world a much better

place for all of us: To my wife and

best friend, Jamie, for her love, patience,

and encouragement. I am indeed the

lucky one. To my mother, who, from

the very start, nurtured my passion for

nature. Thanks, Mom, for tolerating my

propensity for frogs and salamanders.

8

ACKNOWLEDGMENTS

I want to thank a host of folks who provided encouragement, inspiration, and assistance: John Netherton, Mary Taylor Gray, Helen Hickman (the best twin sister in the world), Aaron Salvesen, Nancy Ailes, Randy Rutan, Leslee McCarty, Linda Smith, George Constanz, John Northheimer, Paul Trianosky, Matt Crum, and Rodney Bartgis. I also want to thank everyone I met on the trails, along the rivers, at the overlooks, and in the country stores who provided information, an entertaining story (or a tall tale), or just a smile. A special thanks goes to Alton Byers and Rex Linville of the Mountain Institute, for their support during the project. I am very thankful to them for allowing me to stay at the Institute's Spruce Knob campus during my photo shoots to the area. There is something nice about taking a warm shower after a long day of photography.

Grateful acknowledgment is extended to the Virginia Book Company, Berryville, Virginia, for permission to reprint quotes from *Annals of Blackwater and the Land of Canaan (1746–1880)* by Stuart E. Brown Jr., first published in 1959.

Finally, I want to express a heartfelt thanks to John Fielder, Linda Doyle, Harlene Finn, and Kiki Sayre from Westcliffe Publishers, editor Sallie Greenwood, and designer Rebecca Finkel. Thanks for believing in this project.

WILD GERANIUMS, POCAHONTAS COUNTY

Contents

FOREWORD

On October 18, 1997, I attended the opening dedication of the U.S. Fish and Wildlife Service's National Conservation Training Center (NCTC), Shepherdstown, West Virginia. Situated among rolling hills and meadows along the Potomac River, this 500-acre campus is destined to be the foremost conservation training facility in the world. The center's staff celebrated the dedication with an open house, complete with tours, guest speakers, exhibits, music, and presentations.

One of the program highlights, "A Natural Celebration," was a nature photography presentation given by Jim Clark, chief of the center's wildlife training program. Jim is a highly talented and dedicated nature photographer who spends most of his spare time capturing images which best express his passion for wildlands and wildlife. In order to share his excitement and reacquaint others with our natural heritage, he created "A Natural Celebration."

I was fortunate to see Jim's photography at the NCTC dedication. While viewing his work I realized that a strong new voice for conservation was among us. I also sensed a spiritual journey. The images of the land became holy. I remembered words from Robert Frost's poem, "The Gift Outright," given at President John F. Kennedy's inauguration in 1961:

SANDSTONE CLIFFS,

NORTH FORK MOUNTAIN

The land was ours

Before we were the land's.

In Jim's photographic images we feel love for the land, and we disturb nothing. The program was an inspirational journey through the eyes of a photographer who has a love affair with the natural world.

One segment of the program, called "Highland Overture," was especially compelling. It took us on a seasonal journey through the Allegheny Mountains of eastern West Virginia, a unique region of the Appalachians.

A native son who has rediscovered his home state, Jim has captured on film the essence of what makes this region of West Virginia special with its exceptional landscapes, flowers, and wildlife.

Jim's love for nature and his passion for photography are contagious. I should know, having traveled the world with my late husband, Roger Tory Peterson, who also evoked powerful emotions. Roger spent a lifetime exciting others about our natural world. His books, paintings, and photographs were the catalyst for many young people to pursue a career in protecting and conserving wildlands and wildlife. One of the impressionable young people was Jim. I am proud that his first book about nature was Roger's *A Field Guide to the Birds.* This was the spark that ignited Jim's passion for the natural world. For the past twenty-two years he has dedicated his life as both an accomplished biologist and nature photographer.

For the millions of people who were touched by Roger's love and passion for birds and nature, I am especially pleased and reassured that Jim and others like him will continue the legacy of Roger—a legacy of sharing with all of us the wonderment of our nation's natural heritage. Through the photography in this book, we hope sparks will be ignited in others to convey a sense of place in lesser-known but special regions of our nation.

The Allegheny Highlands of West Virginia is a special place, full of beauty and mystery, an area worthy of our attention. Jim has bestowed a special gift to not only the state of West Virginia, but to everyone who has hiked its winding trails, climbed its ancient mountains, and floated its rushing rivers. This book, *West Virginia: The Allegheny Highlands,* will help create awareness, foster understanding, and generate support for the protection of like areas throughout the country. Future generations will reap the rewards.

I invite you now to take a journey through the mountains, forests, and valleys, and along the rivers of the Allegheny Highlands. Once you have viewed these images, I'm sure you'll be planning a visit to explore these mountains, and you will see why West Virginia is called "Almost Heaven."

—Virginia Marie Peterson
Old Lyme, Connecticut, January 23, 1998

INTRODUCTION

A friend once told me that she loved to go to a marsh in spring, sit back, and let it tell her all its stories. Watching nature unfold before her was like reading a great novel. For a lifetime I have watched a great novel tell me its stories in a unique region of eastern West Virginia. This novel weaves an unending number of seasonal chapters and sagas. A natural classic, the chapters I've experienced have been extraordinary:

SPRING ALONG THE HIGHLAND SCENIC HIGHWAY. The pastel colors decorating the mountain slopes to the east of the highway are too irresistible to pass up. I walk to the edge of the highway, set up my camera, and start capturing on film the essence of an Allegheny spring. While composing the scene, I notice something moving on the right side of my viewfinder. Using a telephoto lens, I see a black bear climbing a tree. Too far to photograph, but what a sight to see. Earlier today, while on Dolly Sods, I watched a family of bobcats play among boulders below Bear Rocks. I wonder what awaits around the next bend of the road.

SUMMER IN THE BLACKWATER CANYON, JUST BELOW BLACKWATER FALLS. The journey from the canyon rim to the river below is not for the faint of heart. The laurel and rhododendron thickets are so dense that I should be able to walk on top of them. The vegetation is so thick that it prevents me from seeing more than a few feet. As I get closer to the river's edge, the air comes alive with mist and the music of wind and the pounding of water on rock. Finally reaching the riverbank, the sight of the river plunging over the falls and rushing down the narrow canyon leaves me speechless.

AUTUMN IN THE OTTER CREEK WILDERNESS. The brilliant colors and sweet aromas of an autumn forest are intoxicating, making me wish this season would never end. The trail is adorned

---

THE PASSAGE OF THE PATOWMAC

THROUGH THE BLUE RIDGE IS

PERHAPS ONE OF THE MOST

STUPENDOUS SCENES IN NATURE . . .

THIS SCENE IS WORTH A VOYAGE

ACROSS THE ATLANTIC.

— *Thomas Jefferson, 1785*

with red and yellow maple leaves from trees edging the river, and while hiking I am well aware that this 20,000-acre

wilderness of hardwood forest and orchid-rich bogs is also a sanctuary for the black bear. I long for a glimpse of the

creek's namesake among the massive boulders in the waterway, and although the chances are slim, just the thought of

what this special place protects is enough to make the journey memorable.

WINTER IN THE SMOKE HOLE CANYON DURING A SNOWSTORM. The first thing I notice about

this snowstorm is how still it is. Nothing is moving; the only sound I hear is the wind

whispering through the trees. Large, soft snowflakes paint the landscape, transform-

ing it into a winter wonderland. I am reminded of how unique this canyon

is, because it is habitat for some of the rarest plant species in the

Appalachian Mountains. Some old-timers call the canyon Smoke

Holes and claim Indians used the caves for smoking

meat. Others say the name came from the smoke

of moonshiners' stills. Regardless, this rugged

canyon is one of the most beautiful places in

the state.

I can only imagine the new chapters

that I will experience in the days to come.

Nestled in the eastern reaches of West Virginia

lies one of the nation's best-kept secrets: the Allegheny

Highlands. The Highlands embrace a landscape of wind-swept

mountains, cascading waterfalls, steep gorges, and picturesque valleys. Though these mountains are ancient and

worn, they are covered with a lush growth of hardwood forests, and the valleys and coves of this region sing with a

thousand streams and rivers. Rivers rise here: the 167-mile-long Greenbrier River, one of the longest free-flowing

rivers in the east, and branches of the Potomac and the New River, an old river.

The Allegheny Highlands of West Virginia is a special region within the Appalachian Mountains. Parts of the region are known locally as the Highland Trace, the Potomac Highlands, and the Alleghenies. I struggled with how to define my coverage and, after talking with ecologists familiar with West Virginia, decided, with their blessing, to use Allegheny Highlands. It is a land of incredible raw beauty—a place that is big enough to become lost in, if you want to. The Highlands border three physiographic provinces. To the east lies the Ridge and Valley, with its series of long mountains and broad valleys. The Allegheny Plateau, with its collection of rolling mountains and deep valleys, occupies the western portion of the Highlands. In between the Plateau and the Highlands is the Allegheny Front, which defines the character of the forests on either side of it. West of the Front, forests are primarily cherry, birch, and maple, while on the east, forests, which are in a rain shadow, are mostly oak, hickory, and pine.

More than one million acres of the Highlands are within the boundaries of two national forests, several state parks and forests, and the nation's 500th national wildlife refuge. The rural charm of this region is enhanced by covered bridges, grist mills, old stone churches, Civil War battlefields, and a host of mountain communities, such as Franklin, Elkins, and the Swiss settlement of Helvetia. Along the Highlands' northeastern boundary is historic Harpers Ferry, where abolitionist John Brown and his cohorts' raid on the federal armory in 1859 ignited events leading to the Civil War in 1861.

Located within an easy day's drive of twenty major eastern cities, this mountain sanctuary offers an alternative for folks weary of competing for solitude and solace at popular and usually crowded national parks in the East. The Highlands have become a destination for outdoor enthusiasts to rejuvenate the body and soul and to revel in the splendor of nature.

These mountains were a source of inspiration and escape to me as a child living in War, a small coal-mining community in southern West Virginia. Each day after school I would dash out the door, and with binoculars in hand, hike into the mountains to roam the slopes and coves until the sun dipped below the horizon. At the age of ten I began a lifelong quest to learn about birds, flowers, trees, and whatever other natural treasures the mountains harbored. The quest has not been completed, nor do I expect it ever will. And, although I left the state for fifteen years, the mountains had captured my heart and entice me back like an old friend.

For this book, I embarked on a journey to portray the allure of the Allegheny Highlands. The experience has strengthened and renewed my passion for our country's natural heritage. Having grown up where strip-mining, water pollution, and blatant disregard for our natural world once ran rampant, I feel lucky to have witnessed the strength these mountains possess to have endured such an unforgiving and relentless onslaught. Although interests intent on exploiting these mountains for personal gain still exist, there are growing numbers of individuals and organizations committed to ensuring that the mountains are never again compromised by the short-term goal of personal profit.

I hope this photographic celebration of the beauty and mystery of the mountains, valleys, and rivers within West Virginia's Allegheny Highlands stimulates others to discover the importance of becoming reacquainted with the land. Places such as the Highlands help us become immersed in the intricacies of the land, its creatures, and the interplay between the two. This in turn instills a passion, an understanding of how important these places are, whether for recreation, for sustaining a local economy, for biological reasons, or simply for the pure joy of knowing these special places exist.

I want this book to serve as a catalyst to inspire you to become a voice for the lesser-known but unique areas of our country, and hope the images reflect why those who call this region home are proud. If they are like me, they cherish the values and treasures these mountains give us. For those finding the Allegheny Highlands a place of refuge from the pressures of living and working in the city, I hope my images conjure pleasant memories of trips past and motivate you to return. For those not yet having experienced this part of West Virginia, I hope the photographs kindle an interest and curiosity that will only be satisfied by a visit.

I have taken a seasonal approach to the book. During my wanderings through the Highlands, I found each season worthy of attention and exploration. Like the mountains themselves, the seasons will share their secrets, but only to those willing to leave the comforts of home and willing to take the time to explore the valleys, rivers, and forests.

PATTERNS OF SPRING

Today is May 15, and although it's the middle of spring, I notice the mountains surrounding Petersburg to the south are dusted with snow. How much I don't know, but from here it appears it won't be too cold up there. I decide to drive the winding dirt road up to Dolly Sods to witness this springtime winter wonderland.

Halfway up the mountain more than three inches of snow cover the ground. How ironic to see this wintry landscape with all the snow and cold whipping about, while at the same time hearing the melodious songs of robins, black and white warblers, and ovenbirds as they stake out their nesting territories. The birds, having just returned from their tropical wintering retreats thousands of miles to the south, must be just as amazed at this snow as I am. This must be winter's last laugh.

Reaching the summit I experience the wind's intensity; it's aggressive, relentless, and forceful. Its power bends many of the red spruce almost to the ground. Leaving the comfort of my vehicle, I walk a few hundred feet to experience the force of the wind. Big mistake. I have never felt such energy in the wind; not just gusts, but a continuous, pounding blast that doesn't subside for several minutes. The wind is so strong I must kneel to clamber back to the vehicle, or I would otherwise be tossed to the ground. All this time the juncos, robins, and sparrows seem not to have a care in the world. In fact, I am sure they are entertained at my predicament. To add insult to injury, a lone raven swoops by effortlessly, croaking its amusement at me. Now I understand why the spruce on the Sods are called flag trees: they have branches only on the leeward side, because the wind and cold temperatures prevent branches from growing on the windward side. This is the coldest I've ever felt in the middle of May.

WE MET WITH A SYCAMORE . . . OF A MOST EXTRAORDINARY SIZE, IT MEASURING THREE FEET FROM THE GROUND, FORTY-FIVE FEET ROUND, LACKING TWO INCHES; AND NOT 50 YARDS FROM IT WAS ANOTHER, THIRTY-ONE FEET ROUND.

—*George Washington*
November 4, 1770

BIG RUN, NEAR CHERRY GROVE, PENDLETON COUNTY

The annual cycle of life in the Allegheny Highlands is played out through four distinct seasons, each desperately holding on as long as it can before the next season claims dominance and reigns for its entitled period. Combined, the seasons of the Highlands create a four-act play with each boasting its own special cast of characters, colors, aromas, and sounds. In the valleys, unlike what I experienced on top of Dolly Sods, the seasons make a more orderly transition from one to another.

BLUE JAY

For the Allegheny Highlands, the eastern phoebe, which arrives in March while winter still retains its grip on the land, is the harbinger of spring. A nondescript bird, the phoebe's emphatic *phee-be* is a welcome start to nature's soon-to-be-growing spring symphony. And although snow may still be blanketing the ground and an impending late winter blizzard may be just around the corner, the phoebe's arrival to the valleys is a reminder for winter to start fading away.

Urged by the warming rays of the sun, spring finally enters the scene. Snowmelt feeds the rivers and streams, creating thundering cascades of waterfalls. Before long, spring begins to decorate bare mountainsides with patterns of fresh colors. As temperatures rise and steady rains coax tree buds to burst forth, hues shift from the somber gray and brown of winter into vibrant green, white, and pink. Spring's paintbrush embellishes the hillsides and mountain slopes until the entire landscape is green from top to bottom.

Spring is enhanced by a rainbow of wildflowers. Dogtooth violet, geranium, bluebell, trillium, and spring beauty dot the forest floor, and add their color to the slopes and valleys. Clumps of ferns unfurl their leaves, and the migration of warblers through the forest brings flashes of color and melodies to the mountains. Ponds, puddles, and lakes become boisterous with the calls of the wood frog, spring peeper, and American toad, and as spring reaches a crescendo, wobbly-kneed white-tailed deer fawns venture carefully along the edges of field and forest.

MOUNTAINS AND VALLEYS

SOUTHWEST OF PETERSBURG,

PENDLETON COUNTY

EARLY SPRING,

HIGHLAND SCENIC HIGHWAY,

POCAHONTAS COUNTY

PASTURE NEAR LINWOOD,

POCAHONTAS COUNTY

LOST RIVER STATE PARK

Along higher elevations, such as Dolly Sods, spring is delayed just a little. Dolly Sods, situated on the escarpment of the Allegheny Front and with elevations ranging from 2,600 to more than 4,000 feet, is a wind-swept plateau with extensive flat rocky plains, upland bogs, flagged spruce, heath barrens, and sweeping vistas. Spring is late here, but when it does happen, it's worth the wait. In late spring Dolly Sods becomes cloaked with beds of bleeding heart, and as spring fades into summer, brilliant displays of azaleas, laurel, and rhododendron grace the landscape.

Surrounded on all sides by hardwood forests, the plant life and climate on Dolly Sods resembles northern Canada, and many species found here are near the limit of their southernmost range. Referred to as "a bit of Canada gone astray," this is a land of black bear and fisher, bog rosemary and yellow-fringed orchid, snowshoe hare and bobcat, cranberry and sundew. But the openness of this unique ecosystem wasn't always so.

Today's Dolly Sods is a result of logging virgin forests, which then altered the ecosystem. The history of the Sods is a microcosm of the story of the Allegheny Highlands. Like the snowstorm I witnessed this spring day, these mountains have weathered many storms since they were formed, but rain, wind, and snow were nothing compared to the onslaught and pounding they experienced from exploitation by humans. In spite of the devastation, these mountains today, like the rebirth of the landscape during spring, have been given another opportunity to reclaim their former natural glory. The history of how the area was relentlessly abused illustrates the resiliency of these mountains and forests.

SOUTH BRANCH OF

THE POTOMAC RIVER,

PENDLETON COUNTY

The first settlers into the Allegheny Highlands encountered a wilderness full of danger and mystery—"a country swarming with wolves and wildcats," as nineteenth-century naturalist Alexander Wilson described it. Although they found the land too rugged and steep for farming, many remained and settled along the fertile floodplains. People came here by choice, not chance, and they sought an independent lifestyle that set them apart from the rest of the eastern settlements.

The first Europeans to visit witnessed a land of towering red spruce, hemlock, and balsam fir. The earliest written record of Dolly Sods was the 1746 diary of Thomas Lewis, a surveyor who was establishing the boundary of

EARLY SPRING,

HIGHLAND SCENIC HIGHWAY,

POCAHONTAS COUNTY

WILD MUSTARD,

HARDY COUNTY

Lower falls,

Falls of Hills Creek

Scenic Area

Lord Fairfax's Virginia estate. The forests surrounding the Sods were a mix of sugar maple, American beech, black cherry, and yellow birch. Along the ridge tops and mountain streams and on hillsides were impenetrable thickets of laurel and rhododendron. Forests of red spruce, interspersed with glades and bogs, covered the higher summits above 3,000 feet.

The red spruce forests must have been spectacular. A conifer more at home in the northern boreal ecosystem than among the hardwoods of the Appalachians, red spruce were nonetheless very common along the higher ridges of the Allegheny Highlands. Trees of ninety feet or more with diameters up to four feet were described by early surveyors, including George Washington, and explorers. Until the mid-to-late 1800s these forests remained intact. Estimates of the red spruce within West Virginia ranged from 400,000 to more than 600,000 acres. With deep layers of rich organic matter on the forest floor, these forests were often described as some of the finest virgin red spruce in the entire eastern United States and quite possibly the world.

PINK LADY'S SLIPPERS,

HAMPSHIRE COUNTY

Through the 1800s, the Highlands, as much of the rest of West Virginia, remained isolated and sparsely populated. The timber resources were used to meet local needs only. Change came slowly to these mountains, but between 1880 and 1920, they would be changed forever—a profound transformation unequal anywhere else in the world at the time.

The agricultural tradition of the region was abruptly altered with the invention of the Shay steam locomotive, a low-gear engine capable of climbing steep grades. With the Shay engine, timber barons had the capability of exploiting every slope and ridge top for its timber. For West Virginia, that meant more than ten million acres of virgin forest. The vast forests of the Alleghenies were no longer inaccessible, and as the forest resources of other regions of the United States diminished, the logging industry turned its attention to West Virginia.

After gandy dancers laid narrow-gauge railroad tracks for the Shays, it didn't take long for loggers called wood hicks to strip whole mountainsides of trees. Wherever there was a forest, from the highest summits to the lowest river valleys, loggers would be there to take it. Within a span of only forty years, practically every acre of forest land in West Virginia had been cut. Estimates of the total board feet taken during this time ranged up to thirty billion board feet. After the devastation one logger boasted, "We didn't leave a stick standing." One newspaperman described the scene as a "monotonous panorama of destruction," while another reported the Highlands as a "forlorn sea of stumps." Even the West Virginia Conservation Commission lamented that the state had not done much for its landscape, "except to mark, mutilate, and burn it up."

But the removal of timber wasn't the end to the devastation. Because the forest canopy had been removed, the forest floor with its accumulation of slash and thick, drying forest duff, became a tinderbox just waiting for a spark to ignite an inferno. And ignite it did. In 1908 alone, seven hundred fires burned more than 1.7 million acres, or 11 percent of the state's area. In 1914, three miles above the logging community of Hendricks, a wildfire broke out

LARGE-FLOWERED TRILLIUM,

BERWIND LAKE

in May that burned until November when heavy snows finally snuffed out the flames. "The sky over Hendricks was lighted with the reflection of the blaze," a writer reported, "that one could sit on the platform of Harvey's store at midnight and read the afternoon paper without any other illumination."

The annihilation of the forests and the subsequent wildfires, soil erosion, and flooding led to the establishment of the Monongahela National Forest—the most important conservation action ever taken in the state. After receiving national forest designation in 1920, subsequent acquisitions have increased the size of the forest to its present-day 910,000 acres. Another 100,000 acres are encompassed within units of the George Washington National Forest. From the start there were efforts to reforest denuded mountain slopes. It is hard to imagine that these mountains with their lush growth of forests were bare, muddy hillsides just seventy years ago.

Today, the primary users of the forests are recreationists, including hunters, anglers, backpackers, hikers, photographers, rock climbers, kayakers, and canoeists. These individuals, who are increasing in number every day, value these mountains not for what they can take from them, but for what the mountains can give them—a sense of adventure and challenge, a place to watch nature's dramas unfold, or just a place to replenish the spirit and celebrate the wonders of nature. Unlike the generation of gandy dancers and wood hicks before them, these folks value the tangible and intangible benefits of protecting watersheds, of holding the land in trust, and of wisely using the resources these mountains and forests offer.

North fork
of south branch,
Potomac River
at Seneca Rocks

30

Rhododendron,

Babcock State Park

POCAHONTAS COUNTY

Spider web

MAIDENHAIR FERN

WHITE-TAILED DEER,

CANAAN VALLEY

CANAAN VALLEY

NATIONAL WILDLIFE REFUGE,

TUCKER COUNTY

Nature of Summer

One warm summer morning my good friends, Nancy Ailes and George Constanz, invited me to photograph the wildflowers flourishing on their farm in Hampshire County. I arrived before daybreak. We sat on the back porch enjoying warm cups of coffee and watched the dawning of a new day. It was a classic summer morning in the Allegheny Highlands. Thick fog draped the mountains and remained suspended like a warm quilt over the valley. Spider webs, meticulously spun along the fence in the meadow, hung heavy with dew, each drop clinging to the strands like a diamond pendant on a thin silver necklace. Treetops stirred with the whispers of a warming breeze, and the sky became a canvas painted with the morning colors of the rising sun. Like most, this morning was nothing short of beautiful.

Instead of exploring the farm, we went to a small pond just a mile down the road. Nancy had discovered some brilliant red cardinal flowers growing along the pond's shoreline. The pond, located in the middle of a meadow, wasn't anything spectacular, just your typical farm pond. But for most of that morning we explored every inch of its verdant shoreline, searching and finding an endless variety of subjects to capture on film—from cardinal flowers, to orb spiders and their dew-covered webs, to bumble bees gathering nectar from bright pink thistles. As soon as we were ready to pack up and leave, we would discover another subject to photograph. It wasn't Yellowstone or the Great Smoky Mountains, but for me, this pond was a Serengeti of life. It brought home that the wonders of nature can be found just outside your door, if you only take the time to look. And it's even better if the doorstep leads into the Allegheny Highlands.

The wonders of the Highlands extend into the evening as well. At day's end, as the sun dipped below the mountains and darkness reclaimed the sky, I headed home. But I pulled off to

SUNRISE, WILLIAMS RIVER, POCAHONTAS COUNTY

THE SUN BY THIS TIME HAD RISEN HIGH ABOVE THE MOUNTAINS, AND WAS SHINING DOWN UPON THE CANAAN WITH ALL HIS REFULGENCE. THE RIVER WAS EVER TURNING IN ITS COURSE, AND EVERY FEW MOMENTS SOME NEW CHARM OF SCENERY WAS GIVEN TO OUR VIEW. THE ATMOSPHERE WAS SOFT AND PLEASANTLY WARM, AND THE BREEZE GENTLY FANNED THE TREES. THE WILDERNESS WAS RICH EVERYWHERE WITH HUES OF ALL DYES, AND THE BANKS OF THE RIVER GLEAMED FOR MILES WITH THE FLOWERS OF THE RHODODENDRON. A SCENE OF MORE ENCHANTMENT IT WOULD BE DIFFICULT TO IMAGINE.

—*Phillip Pendleton Kennedy,*
circa 1853

SUNSET, NEAR SPRUCE KNOB

the side of the highway a few miles from their farm to listen to the night's summer symphony. The musical trills of gray tree frogs pierced the evening air, and a soft summer wind drifting through the valley brought a slight, but welcome chill to the night air. Fireflies illuminated the meadows in front of me, while katydids and crickets added their endless chirping opinions to the world. In the Highlands each moment of the day and night becomes a wonderful mountain memory.

There is no better season than summer to experience the tremendous variety of life in the Allegheny Highlands. Throughout its warm days a procession of wildflowers of every conceivable color and shape decorate the fields and roadsides. Monarch butterflies and American painted ladies pause at each flower, exploring every bloom for nectar. The forests become busy communities of songbirds rearing their young. Turtles bask on logs floating in ponds, while above the water's surface dragonflies conduct aerial assaults on the insect population. Even in the waning days of August, ironweed and joe-pye weed add an additional flash of purple, orange, and pink to the landscape, serving as reminders that summer's end is close at hand.

JOE-PYE WEED,

LOCUST CREEK

In 1853 Phillip Pendleton Kennedy described the Highlands as: "A wilderness of broken and rugged mountains . . . a perfect a wilderness as our continent contained . . ." During this time the Highlands still harbored wolves, elk, and cougars. In *The Blackwater Chronicle,* Kennedy wrote that the Highlands was "a country where the wild beasts of the forest yet roamed unmolested." Much has changed in the Highlands since Kennedy explored and wrote about them in the early 1850s, but these mountains still harbor an amazing diversity of wildlife. When hiking through the virgin hemlock forests of Cathedral State Park in Preston County and the virgin spruce forest of the Gaudineer Scenic Area in Pocahontas County, it's easy to imagine the wildlife and plants that explorers like Kennedy must have witnessed. My first hike in Gaudineer, a 130-acre tract of virgin timber located just below the summit of 4,445-foot Gaudineer Knob, transported me to a time when forests such as this covered nearly ten million acres of West Virginia. Although the tract is small, there are 350-year-old red spruce that are more than one

40

Above: Barn, Randolph County

Right: Roadside near Red Creek, Tucker County

hundred feet high. To visit such a place as this is a spiritual experience. With a light drizzle saturating the fern-draped forest floor and thick fog drifting over portions of the tract, my hike was the type that tickles a photographer's heart, whether or not an image is ever taken. I savored every scene that appeared around each curve of the trail. As the song of a veery floated through the mist-shrouded forest, I discovered a red-spotted newt in its red-eft stage resting on a moss-covered log along the trail. For the next hour I kept company with this remarkable creature, not only to photograph it, but mostly just to watch it.

Some of the creatures Kennedy encountered during his explorations no longer roam the Highlands. Once common along the major river valleys, the last recorded bison was shot near Valley Head in Randolph County in 1825, and by 1890 elk were gone from these mountains. The wolf, an animal Kennedy frequently encountered, disappeared by 1900. As the red spruce forests were logged, so went the porcupine, and with the demise of the majestic chestnut tree by an exotic blight, and the senseless slaughter of the passenger pigeon by market hunters, these two species are also now just Highland memories.

GARDEN (ORB) SPIDER

Some species that came close to becoming extirpated in the Highlands are now common, thanks to conservation efforts to protect them. From a low of only 400 in the 1960s, the population of black bears in the state now exceeds 4,000. White-tailed deer and turkey, two species extremely rare at the turn of the nineteenth century, now flourish throughout the Highlands, and beaver, fisher, and river otter have been successfully re-introduced.

The Highlands harbor a diversity of life; species from all points of the compass mingle here. Birds are a good example. About 300 species of birds occur in the Highlands. In the spruce forests blanketing the summit of Gaudineer Knob alone, you can see twenty-two species of breeding warblers. For many bird species the Highlands are the northernmost or southernmost limit of their range—an exciting situation for naturalists, but for birders, this can create a real challenge. At times the songs coming from the forest can lead one to assume the habitat is strictly a northern forest, but then a southern voice emanates from the same spot, and the assumption is southern forest. Among cardinals, yellowthroats, and wood thrushes, one can also hear and see Swainson's thrushes, Nashville warblers, and northern waterthrushes, species more typical of the boreal forests of Canada. "Delightfully confusing," is how the late Appalachian naturalist Maurice Brooks once described this bird-watching dilemma.

Morning Fog,

Greenbrier Valley,

Pocahontas County

For other species the diversity is equally impressive. Of the forty-two species of amphibians found in West Virginia, twenty-five occur in the Allegheny Highlands, and one, the endangered Cheat Mountain salamander, occurs only at elevations above 3,000 feet in four counties within the Highlands. More than one hundred species of trees occur here, and several of the state's twenty orchid species thrive in these mountains.

The rich assortment of plants and animals is attributable to the last Ice Age. Although glaciers never reached the area, the effects of massive ice sheets were felt nonetheless. Many species migrated south to escape the cold climate and found refuge along the higher and cooler elevations of the Allegheny Highlands. As the glaciers receded, these species remained. On North Fork Mountain, a tract of white birch grows several hundred miles south of its common range, and the snowshoe hare, a species more common two hundred miles north in the Pocono Mountains of Pennsylvania, survives as a relict population in the higher elevations of the Highlands.

WIDOW DRAGONFLY

Another example of rich biological diversity can be seen at the New River Gorge National River. Now a unit of the National Park System, the New River Gorge is a steep canyon in southern West Virginia. The gorge averages 1,000 feet deep, and the New River flowing through it is considered to be second only to the Nile as the oldest river in the world. The gorge and river became a corridor for many species of plants and animals migrating from the advancing Ice Age. Today, the gorge's cool ridges and moist coves still serve as places of refuge for species you would expect to see in Canada, not in southern West Virginia. Who would imagine that one could be scolded by a red squirrel hiding in a hemlock tree in southern West Virginia? The diversity of plant species in the gorge was further enriched after the Ice Age by a northward migration of southern species, such as climbing fern and fringetree.

The most fascinating example of how the Ice Age affected the diversity of plants and animals in the Highlands lies deep in the forest wilderness of Pocahontas County. One of the most remote regions in the east, and a few square miles smaller than the state of Rhode Island, Pocahontas County has one of the largest wilderness areas in the east: the 35,000-acre Cranberry Wilderness, a land of broad and massive mountains rising between 2,400 and 4,600 feet. Skirting the edge of the wilderness is the Cranberry Glades, one of the most uncommon wetland systems found in the country. When walking along the boardwalk that meanders through the glades,

BLACKWATER FALLS

46

Eastern hemlock

and wood fern,

Gaudineer Scenic Area

HEMLOCK FOREST,

CATHEDRAL STATE PARK

THE VIEW WEST

FROM SPRUCE KNOB

it is easy to imagine that you are in the northern reaches of the Alaskan Arctic. With white-tufted cotton grass dotting the glades in autumn, the illusion is even more imaginable.

Situated at an elevation of 3,300 feet and ringed by mountains rising above 4,000 feet, the Cranberry Glades consist of a system of relict bogs covered with a spongy mat of *Sphagnum* moss and a deep layer of peat. With the water table just below the surface, the moss serves as a good insulator, keeping the water relatively cool even in summer. Cool air flowing from the surrounding mountains collects in the glades, adding to the natural refrigeration of these wetlands. For those northern plant species such as northern coralroot and Oswego tea, that migrated south to escape the advancing glaciers, the Cranberry Glades became a home away from home. After the glaciers retreated, these species remained.

For the past 10,000 years the glades have harbored a rich variety of northern plant species, including bunchberry, buckbean, and bog rosemary. The glades are also rich with pink and yellow lady's slippers, purple-fringed, snake-mouth, and grass-pink orchids. In spring the rank odor of skunk cabbage permeates the bog. The carnivorous sundew, a tiny plant that catches and digests insects for protein, also grows here. The thickets of alder and forests of shallow-rooted red spruce and hemlock bordering the glades provide habitat for several northern bird species, including purple finch, alder flycatcher, and northern waterthrush.

CARDINAL FLOWER

The Highland's rich diversity of wildlife and plants is a result of millions of years of climatic and geological occurrences that altered the landscape. Just as these mountains yield an infinite variety of biological delights to the naturalist, the geological treasures found here can keep a geologist busy for several lifetimes. These are some of the oldest mountains in the world, and even today they have stories to be told and mysteries to unravel.

For a mountain boy like myself it's hard to imagine that at one time West Virginia, instead of a landscape of mountains, was part of a vast inland ocean. More than 500 million years ago mountains in the west provided layers of sediment that would eventually fill the ocean. As these layers accumulated, the deposits of sand and silt hardened, eventually forming the thick rock beds occurring in the region today. The actual formation of the

Appalachians occurred about 250 million years ago when the North American continent collided with Africa, causing massive folding, faulting, and uplifting of the bedrock. The Allegheny Highlands, as did much of the Appalachians, had peaks soaring above 15,000 feet, but during the course of several million years the forces of erosion wore these lofty summits down to their present-day modest elevations between 3,500 and 4,861 feet, the elevation of Spruce Knob, the state's highest point.

Throughout the Highlands are hundreds of fascinating geological formations, evidence of how the forces of nature molded this landscape into its present-day form. The most impressive of these formations, Seneca Rocks, is composed of Tuscarora sandstone, which has a higher percentage of quartz than other sandstone types. As the layers of sediment accumulating on the prehistoric ocean floor hardened, the quartz in Tuscarora sandstone became cemented together, resulting in a much harder rock than the layers surrounding it. When the folding and uplifting of the Appalachians occurred, the creation of Seneca Rocks began. As wind and rain wore down the surrounding softer layers of rocks, the sandstone became exposed. Today, Tuscarora sandstone caps most of the ridges in the Highlands.

In 1965, Congress established the 100,000-acre Spruce Knob-Seneca Rocks National Recreation Area, the first designation of this kind to be administered by the U.S. Forest Service, and only one of sixteen such sites in the country. Rock climbers from around the country and around the world come to climb the formation's sheer faces. The crossroads hamlet below the rocks has two rock-climbing schools to prepare the adventurous for an ascent. For those less inclined to experience the cliffs using ropes, there are trails leading to the top.

Seneca Rocks, Cranberry Glades, and New River Gorge are just three of the many natural features that make the Highlands so captivating. Each trip reveals something new to me, and that keeps me coming back, time and again.

HAIR-CAP MOSS

SHAVERS FORK, RANDOLPH COUNTY

ABOVE: FERN ON TREE, SPRUCE KNOB LAKE

RIGHT: VIEW FROM CHIMNEY TOP, NORTH FORK MOUNTAIN

SENECA ROCKS,

PENDLETON COUNTY

YEW CREEK,

CRANBERRY GLADES

BOTANICAL AREA

ABOVE: RED-SPOTTED NEWT

RIGHT: SUNSET, HIGHLAND SCENIC HIGHWAY

HEMLOCKS,

CATHEDRAL STATE PARK

Bear Rocks,

Dolly Sods

TUSCARORA SANDSTONE

CLIFFS AT JUDY GAP,

PENDLETON COUNTY

SENECA ROCKS

AND MORNING FOG

ABOVE: MAPLE TREE BELOW SPRUCE KNOB

LEFT: SOUTH BRANCH VALLEY, HAMPSHIRE COUNTY

ABOVE: PRAYING MANTIS

LEFT: GREENBRIER VALLEY, POCAHONTAS COUNTY

NEW RIVER BRIDGE,

FAYETTE COUNTY

New River,

New River Gorge

National River

ABOVE: MORNING, HIGHLAND SCENIC HIGHWAY

LEFT: SUNRISE FROM NELSON SODS, NORTH FORK MOUNTAIN

COLORS OF AUTUMN

Evening settled over the mountains as the fading light of the day turned the trees surrounding our cabin into silhouettes. With the sun dipping behind the layered ridges, the cool night air coaxed us to retreat inside to the warmth of our cabin. Darkness fell slowly but deliberately as the clouds and the moon grappled for possession of the night. With a fireplace to warm us and a renewed sense of appreciation for nature's handiwork, we reflected on the day spent gazing at the blaze of crimson and gold painted on the mountains.

My mother and I were on our annual pilgrimage through the mountains of West Virginia. For this trip we selected Babcock State Park, just east of the New River Gorge. Our fireside chats during that cool, autumn night revolved around the mountains, and it became clear when we spoke of home, we spoke of the mountains. When the conversation drifted toward the mountains, we spoke of home. It was impossible to discuss one without the other. For anyone who has experienced these mountains, it becomes clear that the Allegheny Highlands weave a special magic for all who come here, whether for a day, a week, or a lifetime. This is a place that can make the spirit soar, and for the Highlands, there is no season better than autumn to ignite the human spirit.

Autumn is nature's grand finale of the year. It's as if autumn has captured the highlights of the previous seasons, mixed them together, and created a visual celebration of nature's best. As the days become shorter and the nights cooler, summer's green becomes autumn's orange, red, and yellow. It's not just the riot of color splashed on every mountain, or the cool, crisp air dispersing the fragrant

MAPLE, PENDLETON COUNTY

> . . . THE EXPEDITION STEPPED OUT ONTO THE FURTHEST VERGE AND VERY PINNACLE OF THE FOAMING BATTLEMENTS, AND GAZED UPON THE SIGHT SO WONDROUS AND SO WILD, THUS PRESENTED TO THEIR ASTONISHED EYES. . . . PERHAPS IN ALL THIS BROAD LAND OF OURS, WHOSE WONDERS ARE NOT YET HALF REVEALED, NO SCENE MORE BEAUTIFULLY GRAND EVER BROKE ON THE EYE OF THE POET, OR PAINTER . . .
>
> —*David Hunter Strother,*
> *circa 1851*

aroma of autumn leaves, or the clear, blue skies that cause this season to be so enticing. It is the blending of all these traits that makes a Highlands autumn so extraordinary.

Leaves begin to change along the higher ridges in early September. The palette of fall colors seeps down the slopes into the valleys. No tree is left unchanged as autumn's paintbrush decorates every leaf with rich tones of gold, orange, and red. But the fall colors are not the only change occurring here. For the Highlands' wild inhabitants, autumn is the time to prepare for winter. For birds, that means the annual fall migration.

For millions of songbirds and raptors, the high summits along the Allegheny Front serve as important corridors during migration. As the heath barrens on Dolly Sods turn into a deep, rich burgundy, an endless parade of warblers, thrushes, and other songbirds pass over the summit for destinations that will be warm during the coming winter months. During my autumn photo trips to the Sods I not only captured images of the colorful fall landscape, but I spent hours watching in amazement as endless flights of birds followed their instincts to go south. During one cool, clear autumn morning, I stood spellbound as flock after flock of blue jays silently passed over me. By noon I had counted more than 2,000 of these azure-feathered migrants flying overhead.

LAKE REFLECTIONS,

WATOGA STATE PARK

Birds are not the only aerial migrants along these summits. In September the blue skies above Dolly Sods are graced with orange clouds of monarch butterflies as they migrate south. Clusters of these elegant migrants congregate on milkweeds, resting and refueling before continuing on their long journey to Mexico.

A great place to watch the annual fall migration on Dolly Sods is at Bear Rocks. Among massive rock formations and boulders you can soak in the vistas to the east while scanning the ridgeline to the north for flocks of migrating birds. This annual parade of migrants over Dolly Sods has not gone unnoticed by ornithologists. Since 1958, from August to October, volunteers have operated a bird-banding station on Dolly Sods. With the use of mist nets, these intrepid bird banders have captured and banded more than 165,000 birds representing more than one hundred species, including Cape May, Blackburnian, and bay-breasted warblers.

MAPLE LEAVES AND STREAM

GLADE CREEK GRIST MILL,

BABCOCK STATE PARK

MIDDLE FALLS,

FALLS OF HILLS CREEK

SCENIC AREA

Of course, the number one attraction for visitors and residents alike is the fall colors, and one of my favorite drives is the Highland Scenic Highway in Pocahontas County. A federally designated scenic highway, West Virginia 39/55 and West Virginia 150 gently wind forty-four miles through the Monongahela National Forest between Richwood and Marlinton, and more than twenty-two miles traverse above 4,000 feet. The highway showcases vistas of hardwood forests, meadows, and river valleys and offers turnoffs and access to trailheads into the 35,000-acre Cranberry Wilderness and the 26,000-acre Cranberry Back Country.

No autumn visit is complete without a trip into Canaan Valley. Situated at 3,200 feet above sea level in eastern Tucker County, Canaan Valley is the highest major mountain valley east of the Mississippi. Within the two-to-four-mile-wide, fourteen-mile-long valley are the headwaters of the Blackwater River that flows northward exiting through a water gap between Canaan and Brown Mountains. The river plunges over sixty-two-foot-high Blackwater Falls and continues its journey through the steep-walled Blackwater Canyon until it flows into the Dry Fork of the Cheat River. The amber color of the Blackwater River comes from leached tannic acids of spruce and hemlock bordering the river.

Legend has it that the name of the valley was coined by George Cassey Harness, a religious sort who loved to hunt bear and spent considerable time exploring this region. Sometime in 1753, Harness stood on Cabin Mountain and, witnessing the valley for the first time, supposedly cried out, "Behold! The land of Canaan!" The pronunciation of Canaan is Kah-NANE—not the Biblical pronunciation of KAY-nan.

MOUNTAIN ASH,

DOLLY SODS

Because of its 3,200-foot elevation Canaan Valley is in a frost pocket where cold air flows down from the surrounding mountains and collects on the valley floor, making frost a possibility any day of the year. The valley maintains its lush character because of frequent fogs, cold temperatures, and abundant rainfall. Autumn comes early to the valley, and the colors displayed here create a fantastic patchwork of brilliant hues. Like Dolly Sods, the valley

BLACKWATER RIVER, BLACKWATER FALLS STATE PARK

78

ABOVE: OTTER CREEK WILDERNESS

RIGHT: LOWER FALLS, FALLS OF HILLS CREEK SCENIC AREA

80

BLACKWATER CANYON,

TUCKER COUNTY

has been described as "a bit of Canada gone astray." The diversity of plant communities, wet soils, and high elevation makes the valley home for many plant and animal species more commonly found in northern New England and Canada. But what really separates Canaan Valley from other eastern mountain valleys is its extensive system of wetlands—the largest intact freshwater complex in the Appalachians. Within the valley's 35,000-acre watershed are more than 8,000 acres of wetlands that provide habitat for a host of wetland-dependent wildlife and plant species.

Canaan Valley is a naturalist's dream. More than 290 species of wildlife are found here, and more than 580 different species of plants have been recorded for the valley, including more than 109 species considered to be boreal in distribution. For balsam fir, highbush cranberry, and swamp saxifrage, Canaan Valley represents the southernmost limit of their range.

When Thomas Lewis explored the Highlands in the 1700s, Canaan Valley was covered with towering red spruce and dense, impenetrable thickets of laurel and rhododendron. While exploring the valley in 1746, Lewis wrote:

> the Dismal appearance of the place Being Sufficen to Strike terror in any human Creative . . . ye Lorals Ivey & Spruce pine so Extremely thick in ye Swamp through which this River Runs that one Cannot have the Least Prospect Except they look upwards the water of the River of Dark Brownish Color & its motion So Slow that it can hardly be said to move.

Even most Native Americans avoided settling here, preferring instead, like the Massawomee tribe of the Iroquois Nation, to visit the valley in search of big game.

Regardless of Lewis's initial description of the valley, as early as 1850, it became a tourist attraction, especially for Europeans seeking a wilderness experience. When the railroads arrived in the 1880s and the lust for the valley's timber became insatiable, however, the character of the valley was changed forever. Between 1880 and 1920, millions of years of biological diversity were nearly erased by loggers. Fortunately the valley still possesses many of the unique characteristics that attracted the first visitors.

AUTUMN GROUND COVER

Instead of "striking terror in any human Creative," Canaan Valley is now one of those gems in the Highlands providing an opportunity to experience the outdoors. More than 1.5 million people visit the valley annually, each participating in a variety of outdoor recreational activities. In 1974, to recognize the beauty and

REFLECTIONS,

SOUTH BRANCH OF THE

POTOMAC RIVER,

GRANT COUNTY

uniqueness of the valley, the Secretary of the Interior designated a portion of Canaan Valley as a National Natural

Landmark. The Department of Interior's evaluation reported that "the total valley is a thing to be experienced . . .

it ranks with Yosemite and Yellowstone Valleys, though not, of course, quite their size. In the east, however, there

are very few areas of its grandeur and magnificence."

Canaan Valley still faces the same problem that beleaguers other areas of such scenic beauty: uncontrolled

development. Ski resorts and vacation and retirement homes, along with the attendant support businesses, have now

sprung up in the valley. And there are still attempts to exploit the valley at the expense of its natural beauty. In the

early 1970s, Allegheny Power Systems, which owns a major portion of the northern region of the valley, proposed

damming the valley. The company planned to generate electricity by using a pump storage technique where water

from a 7,000-acre reservoir in the valley would be pumped up to a facility on top of Cabin Mountain and back

down again. The idea had disaster written all over it, and opposition to the plan effectively thwarted any attempts

for this project to proceed.

In 1997 a private timber company announced plans to log

Blackwater Canyon, one of the most rugged landscapes in the Appalachian

Mountains. The canyon is located just below Blackwater Falls, which David

Strother described in the 1850s as a "sight so wondrous and so wild." The

Blackwater River rushes through the boulder-strewn canyon, dropping

136 feet per mile for eight miles. Logging would effectively destroy the

very thing that attracts a million visitors each year, who bring an estimated

$22.3 million into the local economy. I have yet to see a situation where

people spend that kind of money to marvel at a clearcut.

HAY-SCENTED FERN

Efforts are underway to protect significant tracts of the remaining

untrammeled portions of Canaan Valley. More than 6,000 acres in the southern part of the valley have been set

aside as Canaan Valley State Park, and in 1994 the U.S. Fish and Wildlife Service established the Canaan Valley

National Wildlife Refuge. Though currently fewer than 2,000 acres, there is hope that the refuge will expand to

as many as 25,000 acres, forever protecting the vital wetlands and other unique habitats in the northern reaches

of the valley. By embracing a land ethic that recognizes the value of its wildlands, Canaan Valley and the rest of the

Allegheny Highlands may be able to retain much of the beauty and diversity David Hunter Strother so eloquently

described more than a hundred years ago.

84

SUGAR MAPLE

SUNRISE,

ALLEGHENY TRAIL,

POCAHONTAS COUNTY

MORNING FOG,

TUCKER COUNTY

ALLEGHENY AUTUMN,

POCAHONTAS COUNTY

CANAAN VALLEY

FROM CABIN MOUNTAIN,

TUCKER COUNTY

ABOVE: BLUEBERRY SHRUBS AND BOULDERS

LEFT: BABCOCK STATE PARK

COVERED BRIDGE,

LOCUST CREEK,

POCAHONTAS COUNTY

SENECA ROCKS

ABOVE: HIGHLAND SCENIC HIGHWAY

RIGHT: CHAMPE ROCKS, PENDLETON COUNTY

ABOVE: COTTON GRASS, CRANBERRY GLADES BOTANICAL AREA

LEFT: WETLAND, DOLLY SODS WILDERNESS

98

RIGHT: DROOP MOUNTAIN

BATTLEFIELD STATE PARK

FAR RIGHT: FOREST ROAD,

MONONGAHELA NATIONAL

FOREST

VISION OF WINTER

The silence of this winter morning is such that I can hear my breath being

taken away. Before me is a landscape of rock, snow-draped trees, frozen water,

and parting clouds. The colors of gray and white dominate, interrupted only by

a stand of green hemlock and spruce bordering the river. As dawn breaks, the

sun paints the tops of the mountains. Except for the muffled rushing of water

behind a sheet of ice covering the waterfall in front of me, there is no sound. This

scene of freshly fallen snow embodies the essence of nature in its purest form: simple and

wondrous. Although it is cold, the passion in my heart for nature fuels a warmth that will

keep me comfortable all day.

I am standing in front of Blackwater Falls in Tucker County. A winter storm the previous

day covered the Highlands with more than a foot of snow, which for me was an invitation to leave

the comforts of a warm home to photograph the exquisite beauty of the season. Slipping and sliding

down the snow-crusted trail, I reached the waterfall and spent the morning alone, immersed in

photographing the elegance of all that surrounded me. My only company was flocks of juncos

and chickadees flitting through the trees, occasionally flying near me for a closer inspection. The

sun played hide-and-seek with the clouds, providing opportunities for me to photograph the scene

in a variety of moods. With overcast skies, the snowcovered mountains blended in with the clouds.

When the clouds disappeared, the sky became as blue as the feathers on a blue jay and reflected

deeply on the water's surface, creating a mirage that made it appear there were two skies, one on

top of the other. Like many of the days I've spent photographing in the Highlands, these are the

moments I wish could last forever.

A NATURE LOVER

IS SOMEONE, WHO,

WHEN TREED BY A BEAR,

ENJOYS THE VIEW.

—Anonymous

MORNING, GRANT COUNTY

Many folks dismiss winter, waiting impatiently for the cold and monochromatic landscapes to change once again into the vibrant green of spring and summer. But for me, winter in the Highlands, especially after a fresh snow has covered the land, is just as captivating as the flowers of spring, the warm days of summer, or the colors of autumn. As Henry David Thoreau wrote, "The question is not what you look at, but what you see."

In the Highlands, snow can occur as early as October and as late as May. But November is the time heralding the transition between fall and winter. The season's first snowfall crafts a softly seductive vista of gentle contours and patterns, concealing all evidence of the previous seasons. With just snow and ice, winter fashions simple elemental designs out of the landscape. This exquisite beauty is both obvious and subtle, but even without snow, winter still offers a time for exploration and discovery in the Highlands.

A walk along a forest trail, even in a light drizzle, is a perfect way to experience a winter's day in the Highlands. My many winter hikes around Berwind Lake, a twenty-acre impoundment surrounded by a forest of lush hardwoods near my childhood home, were often the perfect remedies for getting out of the house. I can still remember those walks: The trail is strewn with the wet, fading leaves of autumn that effectively muffle my footsteps.

SYCAMORE BRANCH

As raindrops dance on the surface of the lake, the day appears dreary, but the quiet and solitude of the forest are refreshing. The silence and serenity are broken by the wind through bare branches of hickory trees, the creaking of an old oak tree, and the resounding voice of a pileated woodpecker as it flies through the forest. Beyond the lake are patches of fog, appearing as wandering ghosts enveloping the landscape. A breeze jostles raindrops clinging to tree branches, plunging them onto the forest floor. Like jewels on a necklace, a few drops linger on the branches. A close look in a drop reveals an upside-down panorama of the winter forest.

Winter reveals what spring and summer concealed. Mountain ridges appear as rippling muscles, forming deep V-shaped valleys where small streams flow cold and clear and full with winter's bounty of rain and melting snow. Massive boulders and jagged cliffs hidden in summer are now visible, proof of the geologic age of these once majestic, towering mountains. Scattered on the slopes are hemlocks—lone sentinels of green breaking the expanse of bare hardwoods. The faded hues of Christmas fern poking through the snow add extra color to winter's landscape, and the ashen bark of an old beech tree contrasts sharply with its few remaining tan leaves.

NEAR SNOWSHOE,

POCAHONTAS COUNTY

ABOVE: FROST, DOLLY SODS WILDERNESS

RIGHT: BEECH TREES AND SNOW, POCAHONTAS COUNTY

Blackwater Falls,

Blackwater Falls State Park

Throughout the forest lay fallen trees, former monarchs that evoke days of past majesty, but now provide for the next generation of forest life. Large rectangular holes hewed in the trunk of a snag along the trail mark the work of a pileated woodpecker. And always present during my winter treks are the hardy woodland gang of avian clowns—chickadees, titmice, and nuthatches—that troop through the forest, closely inspecting every disturbance to their domain.

Along the lake's edge, silhouettes of the trees along the bank cast a ghostly reflection in the water. A light breeze ripples the water, bringing the spectral figures to life. Ice rimming the shoreline traps an array of leaves, creating an abstract arrangement of ragged shapes and patterns. Cattails, brown and brittle, stand silent at the far end of the lake, while perched on the far reaches of a branch over the water, a kingfisher patiently watches for the slightest movement in the water—a sure sign of supper. Abruptly, the kingfisher leaps off the branch and cruises to the other side of the lake, hoping its luck may improve.

Each one of my winter treks around the lake has been eventful, full of surprises and discovery. But one hike I shared with my wife, Jamie, a few years ago was especially memorable. We were visiting my mother during the Christmas holidays. Christmas morning was cold with scattered snow flurries. By early afternoon Jamie and I decided to hike around the lake. The snow had stopped, and the temperature, though cold, was perfect for a winter stroll.

A rainstorm the previous night had transformed small tributaries flowing into the lake into rushing streams; some resembled miniature water-falls and caused us to detour from our usual route. Our normal crossing spot at the upper end of the lake was partially submerged, challenging us to do some tricky maneuvering across a narrow log that crossed the stream. Jamie went first and as expected, succeeded with no problem. With my sense of balance obviously lacking, I proved to be of some amusement to her, but nevertheless, I made it without falling.

STAGHORN SUMAC

After completing our hike, we sat on a bench overlooking the lake and watched the day fade into dusk. Within a few minutes, we heard what seemed to be another group of hikers across the lake. Hikers they were; humans they were not. Four turkeys were causing all the commotion, strolling on the snow-crusted leaves just above the trail. They paid no attention to us, moving deliberately along the forest floor and softly clucking among themselves. We watched them for several minutes until they disappeared into a clump of rhododendron. For us, that was a perfect ending to a wonderful winter holiday, and just another natural day in the Allegheny Highlands.

Above: White-tailed deer, Canaan Valley

Left: Lost River State Park

BARN IN SNOWSTORM,

NEAR MARLINTON

Maple and fog,

Randolph County

FROST ON

BLACKBERRY LEAVES,

DOLLY SODS

PENDLETON FALLS,

BLACKWATER FALLS

STATE PARK

BLACKWATER FALLS,

BLACKWATER FALLS STATE PARK

BLACKWATER RIVER

MOUNTAIN SPIRIT

Now it's late October, and from all signs, autumn is coming to an end in the Highlands. This is the last day of my annual photo shoot here, and I can't think of a better way to celebrate than by hiking up to Pike Knob, one of the many sanctuaries managed by the West Virginia Chapter of the Nature Conservancy. Located along the southern terminus of North Fork Mountain, Pike Knob protects the southernmost stand of virgin red pine, a species more commonly found in New England and the northern Great Lakes region.

With a 4 A.M. departure from our base camp at the Mountain Institute's outdoor campus below Spruce Knob, my good friend Aaron Salvesen and I drive to Franklin to meet with Cecelia Mason, a reporter for West Virginia Public Radio. Within minutes we are driving up the dirt road to Pike Knob. When the road becomes impassable, we park and start hiking the final mile to the summit. Our small flashlights are just powerful enough to illuminate the rocky trail in front of us. For the next hour, in near total darkness, we tackle the steep trail, adding to the challenge by lugging backpacks full of camera gear. The autumn air is cool and crisp, and scanning upward I see scattered clouds sweeping the sky.

We reach the summit in time to photograph sunrise. As night becomes day, we are silenced by the beauty of the scene unfolding before us. Reds and violets tint the sky, and the clouds drifting from the west complement the scene. By midmorning a light rain filters down from gray skies. Eventually, we call it a day and, with some reluctance, head home. For most of the drive we are quiet, each reliving the many experiences we have been blessed with since coming here to photograph—pleasant mountain memories forever etched in our minds and hearts.

Throughout the Allegheny Highlands are special places like Pike Knob, places where a person can revel in the mysteries and beauty of nature. These are places to let the human spirit soar and to experience the best in what nature has to offer. More importantly, these places provide a sanctuary for many of the world's unique, rare, and fragile species. As part of the oldest chain of mountains in the world, the diversity found here, as it is elsewhere in the Appalachians, is phenomenal. In every way the Highlands exemplify the best of the world's temperate forests, but unfortunately, in many other ways, humanity's acts inflicted here illustrate the very worst treatment of our wildlands and wildlife. For many, the Highlands are still considered a place to practice Manifest Destiny.

For hundreds of millions of years these mountains accepted the challenges nature imposed upon them. This was to be expected. But for the past hundred years, as unwilling victims of greed, the Highlands have nearly been robbed of all their worth: Mountains cleared of their trees, and water too polluted to drink. Our natural family, the animals and plants that share this world with us, fared worse. No longer do the wolf, the bison, or the elk grace these mountains.

I have witnessed the ability of these mountains to persevere in spite of what society threw at them. But nature can only forgive us and heal its wounds for so long; after that, all is lost, and one more piece of the puzzle that sustains us is gone forever. I struggle with the thought that we could lose the very treasure, our natural heritage, that enriches so many of our lives. I often think of what John Burroughs, Thomas Edison, Henry Ford, and Harvey Firestone saw when they came to the Highlands in the summer of 1918 to fish and camp. The devastation of the region's forest had already occurred by this time, but enough wild areas were still left to entice them to find refuge and solace here. Our legacy should be to ensure the same opportunity for future generations to experience our nation's natural heritage.

The challenges facing the Highlands today are just as threatening as the massive logging that devastated the entire state less than a hundred years ago. And the threats are many: A proposed four-lane highway would cut a 114-mile strip across the upper portion of the Highlands, from Elkins to the Virginia state line. The rapid growth of the poultry industry in the Highlands threatens water quality

AUTUMN MORNING,

HIGHLAND SCENIC HIGHWAY

in the Potomac River and Chesapeake Bay watersheds. One of the most scenic views in the entire eastern United States, the rugged Blackwater Canyon, is currently threatened with logging and vacation-home development, which would destroy the very reason that one million visitors come here each year.

An increasing number of individuals and organizations are watching over these mountains, working to protect them for many tomorrows to come. The West Virginia Chapter of the Nature Conservancy has protected thousands of acres of unique biological communities in the Highlands. As part of its Smoke Hole-North Fork Mountain Bioreserve, the Conservancy is working with private landowners to provide a network of protected areas along the Potomac River's South Branch Valley. This rugged land harbors more than one hundred rare species, including arctic plants that were pushed south during the last ice age.

The Mountain Institute, an international organization headquartered in Franklin, is working to preserve mountain environments around the world, including the Allegheny Highlands. Their 400-acre research and education campus near the summit of Spruce Knob provides the opportunity for young and old alike to learn more about the ecology and culture of the Appalachian Mountain region. Other organizations, such as the Cacapon Institute, the Highlands Conservancy, and local chapters of the Audubon and Sierra Club, are working to protect the region's natural heritage through education, and research, and by invoking actions to challenge threats imposed by others on the integrity of the Highlands. These mountains deserve more than they have received in the past, and with the help of these organizations and others, we will at least be able to speak for the mountains when they are threatened.

Recent studies have shown that tourism and outdoor recreation in the national forests of the southern Appalachians contribute more than $370 million annually to the local economy, as compared to $32 million from logging. Places such as the Allegheny Highlands will be more valuable because an increasing number of visitors want to experience the challenges of hiking a mountain trail, fishing in a mountain stream, or scaling a rock face. And there are those who want to sit down, lean against a tree, and watch the wonders of nature unfurl before them.

SUNRISE FROM NELSON SODS,

NORTH FORK MOUNTAIN

History and the forces of nature met to define the character of the Allegheny Highlands, sometimes for the good, many times for the bad. The Highlands, as with all of West Virginia, is a land of startling beauty, a land with a colorful and tragic past, a struggling and challenging present, and a hopeful tomorrow. The time has come for those who call these mountains home to do more to embrace the true values of what the mountains harbor, to give their wounds, time to heal, and to give them an opportunity to show that they can be as productive without being ravaged as they were a hundred years ago. We all know in our hearts that not every acre has to be cut, nor every river dammed, or every hillside leveled. I doubt the next generation and the generations after them would appreciate us leaving such a legacy for them to handle.

I learned about our kinship to all things natural, wild, and free in the Highlands. The mountains instilled in me a tremendous strength to endure whatever obstacles were placed in my path, and they forged in my heart a passion for life. Not only is this my home, the mountains are my friends. As I have done many times before, I will return from time to time to renew my friendship with them. And as with all my good friends, I hope they will have many more stories to share with me.

For information about the state parks within the Allegheny Highlands, including Babcock, Beartown, Blackwater, Cacapon, Cass Scenic Railroad, Cathedral, Droop Mountain Battlefield, Fairfax Stone, Hawks Nest, Holly River, Lost River, Pipestem, Twin Falls, and Watoga, call (800) 225-5982. Many of the parks have cabins and room accommodations, restaurants, and activities. The Internet site for West Virginia is http://www.wva.com.

The following organizations and agencies can provide information about recreational opportunities and issues in the Highlands.

CACAPON INSTITUTE
Route 1, P.O. Box 328
High View, WV 26808
(304) 856-1100

CANAAN VALLEY NATIONAL
WILDLIFE REFUGE
P.O. Box 1278
Elkins, WV 26241
(304) 637-7312
e-mail: r5rw_cvnwr@fws.gov
http://www.fws.gov/r9realty/
cvalley.html

GEORGE WASHINGTON
NATIONAL FOREST
101 North Main Street
Harrison Plaza
Harrisonburg, VA 22801
(540) 433-2491

MONONGAHELA
NATIONAL FOREST
U.S. Forest Service
200 Sycamore Street
Elkins, WV 26241-3962
(304) 636-1800

THE MOUNTAIN INSTITUTE
P.O. Box 907
Dogwood & Main Street
Franklin, WV 26807
(304) 358-2401
e-mail: summit@igc.apc.org
http://www.mountain.org

THE NATURE CONSERVANCY
OF WEST VIRGINIA
723 Kanawha Boulevard, East
Suite 500
P.O. Box 3754
Charleston, WV 25337
(304) 345-4350

NEW RIVER GORGE
NATIONAL RIVER
National Park Service
P.O. Box 246
Glen Jean, WV 25846-0246
(304) 465-3052

THE SIERRA CLUB–
WEST VIRGINIA CHAPTER
P.O. Box 4142
Morgantown, WV 26504-4142
(304) 363-4006

WEST VIRGINIA HIGHLANDS
CONSERVANCY
P.O. Box 306
Charleston, WV 25321

OTTER CREEK

TECHNICAL NOTES

The photographs for this book were captured with a variety of Nikon cameras, including an F3, F4, N90, and, during the last year of the project, an F5. An assortment of Nikkor lenses were used, including a 20–35mm zoom, 80–200mm zoom, 200mm micro, and 400mm. All images were captured with the camera placed on either a Gitzo model 320 or 410 tripod with an Arca Swiss ball head. Film used was primarily Fuji Velvia, with some Fuji Provia and Kodak Elite. The only filters used were a polarizer, warming, and split-neutral density.